Still Waters

Author at Age Ten—Chippewa River

Still Waters

Timeless Reflections for the Soul

D. J. Christophersen

Cedar Leaf Press
San Antonio, Texas

Cedar Leaf Press
17503 La Cantera Parkway, Suite 104-240
San Antonio, TX 78257

Copyright © 2009 by D. J. Christophersen

All rights reserved. No part of this book may be reproduced or utilized in any form without permission in writing.

The poems *Horizons*, *Trees*, and *A Worm And Her Majesty* were published in *Breakaway: How I Survived Abuse* by Nadia Sahari (2009), Reprinted with the permission of Pink Butterfly Press.

Library of Congress Cataloging-in-Publication Data

Christophersen, D. J. [date]

Still Waters: Timeless Reflections for the Soul

p.   cm.

ISBN 978-0-9820413-3-8 (paper)

Library of Congress Control Number: 2009937621

1. Christophersen, D. J. [date]. 2. Poetry—Nostalgia.
3. Poetry—Christmas. 4. Poetry—Inspiration.

Printed in the United States of America
Printed on acid-free paper

To the memory of Elmer and Clarence, Norwegian gentlemen and true guardians of the forest

Still Waters

Contents

Part One—Nostalgia

Still Waters	15
The Concert	17
The Blackberry Patch	19
Memories	22
A Dweller in the Woods	26
The Genealogist	29

Part Two—Christmas

A Boy's Christmas	37
Christmas Now	45
Marching Pilgrims	50
The Journey	53
The First Christmas	55

Part Three—Inspiration

The Seed	61
The Gallery	64
The Creation	66
God's Promise	69

Still Waters

The Heart of God	72
Horizons	74
A Better Day	76
A Worm And Her Majesty	78
Tadpole Yearnings	83
What Have You Done For Me?	86
Trees	89
Voices	95
A Humble Prayer	98
The Giant Self	99
Sunset	100

Part One

Nostalgia

Still Waters

Still Waters

*Still waters end the rapids
Past the boulders round and bare,
Where the rushing, gushing river
Finds relief from all its care.
It is there in tranquil silence
That the river bends its knee
To meditate and contemplate
Its journey to the sea.
Stillest waters are the deepest,
And the treasures that they hold
Will for those who pause to listen
Reveal secrets yet untold.
It is in the quiet waters
That the river will abide,
In a search for honest answers
All its questions will confide.
What can I take of value
To the ocean vast and wide?*

Still Waters

Will the gifts I bear have meaning
To the everlasting tide?
What course of action shall I take
Within these narrow walls?
Shall I continue slow of pace
Or generate a falls?
Shall I go straightforward on
To reach my final goal?
Or shall I go meandering
And pause at every hole?
No one really knows the future
Of a river or a stream.
In the universe of questions,
Answers always have a seam.
So ever onward flows the river
From its upward starting place
Toward its downward destination
Till it meets it face to face.

Still Waters

The Concert

Nothing much can match the music
Of the frogs in evening croaking.
Across the road and by the field
A choir of frogs is soaking.
The pond is but the runoff
From the melted winter snow,
Where the culvert ends the rivulets
From our hill to down below.
Until May the pond is frozen,
But by June it is no more.
And you know the concert's coming
'Cuz you've heard it all before.
From the porch where we are sitting
On our balcony of wood,
We can hear the choir assembling,
Warming up as any should.
From the youngest voice among them,
Just a tadpole days ago,

Still Waters

To the basso bullfrog grumble
They get ready for the show.
The newest voices sing soprano.
Older altos find their pitch.
Soon the bullfrog's voice is belching
From the teeming, singing ditch.
It is just as evening shadows fall
That the choir is at its best,
In the warm and gentle breezes
When the countryside's at rest.
You can't hear this kind of music
In the city concert halls.
This is music to perfection,
Uninhibited by walls.
It is Nature's finest gathering
Of ensembles made to hop.
It's the kind of water music
That you hope will never stop.

Still Waters

The Blackberry Patch

There was a place, not far from home,
Across the lake named Barker,
Through the woods along the trail
To branches bent as marker.
The older children took the lead
For the little ones to follow.
We all went voluntarily
To a place called Mosquito Hollow.
In a round-bottomed rowboat
Across the lake we ferried.
Lard buckets, dishpans,
And coffee cans we carried.
The August sun bore down upon us,
Long-sleeved shirts and all,
But nothing could dissuade us
From the annual berry call.
The patch was shared by birds and bears
And other friends as well.

Still Waters

On each of us the bounty
Of the Hollow cast its spell.
With briars tearing at our sleeves
And ripping at our trousers,
Happily we staked our claim
Among the other browsers.
We always kept an eye well peeled
In case the bears were near.
We had to be on guard for them
But never out of fear,
But just in case we wandered 'tween
A mother and her cubs
While concentrating only
On the filling of our tubs.
The berries in the Hollow were
As large as half your thumbs.
And they filled our pans as easily
As if they had been plums.
For berries black and juicy do not
Settle in the pan.
And when it's full they're just as good
As they were when you began.
Of course we had to sample some
As we picked along the way.

Still Waters

But because they were so plentiful
We were finished by midday.
With dishpans full and buckets, too
We rowed toward our abode,
Bearing with us fifty quarts
Of berries as our load.
Some berries would be put aside
For cream and sugar treats.
But most were canned the old-fashioned way
And saved for winter feasts
Of jams and jellies spread upon
Hot bread just oven-baked,
While we recalled the August sun
And the claim that we had staked.
I wonder if the berry patch
Still stands in Mosquito Hollow,
Where other folks might find the trail
That we so liked to follow.
If so we'll share fond memories
Of summer days well spent
In a favorite spot across the lake
Where we so often went.

Still Waters

Memories

So long the time now separates us
From that generation gone,
From great minds and souls before us
Whose pioneering work is done.
They remind us that another time
And place can still be got
If we pursue the dreams they had
And the way of life they sought.
There comes to mind the contribution
Of their gentle, homely ways,
Of the simple, humble manner
That they followed all their days.
Like Thoreau at Concord's cabin
Tranquil by his chosen wood,
They besought a quiet lifestyle
Doing only what is good.
I recall with profound pleasure
The way my uncles lived their lives,

Still Waters

Two bachelors choosing nature
As most men would choose their wives.
They lived in true devotion
To an ideal way of life—
Far from city noise and commerce,
Far from turmoil, toil and strife,
In a cabin bare of features
That the outside world desires,
Near their blacksmith shop with billows
And the hardwood for its fires.
There they forged the tools they needed
For the pulpwood that they sold
To the paper mill downriver
From logs drayed in winter's cold.
Two draft horses bore the burden
Of the drayage year by year.
And no two partners, horse and owner,
Could be bound by love more dear.
In total harmony with nature—
Plants and animals combined—
They served the forest as custodians,
Always gentle, good, and kind.
I saw wild birds and squirrels wary
Come to them without a fear.

Still Waters

I saw raccoons and lynx and bobcats
Come to them just like the deer.
The forest creatures seemed to know
That with these men there was no harm,
And so they came unthreatened
Like the animals on a farm.
Today such men are rare indeed
In our world fast-paced and cruel.
How much better would our world be
If we lived their gentle rule.
Still we hope that when our time to leave
This busy world has passed,
We shall leave behind us memories
Like the ones that they have cast.
I miss everything about these men
Who lived for peace and love,
And I know they live eternally
In the Forest up above.
Our journey will move on apace
And when the time is right,
We'll join them in their travels
Through a universe that's bright
With hope and joy to mark our way
As branches that they bent

Still Waters

*Along the trail to guide us
As a message that they sent.
"Be kind," they said, "and humble
At the knee of Mother Earth,
For she's the gracious lady
That has guided you since birth.
Do not abuse what she has lent —
Use only what you need.
Do think of others after you
And spare them all your greed.
Love all the creatures of the earth
And give them what is due,
For life is surely better
If it's not lived all for you."*

Still Waters

A Dweller in the Woods

Nature has its epic tales
Of ocean storms and giant whales,
Of turtles green that travel wide
On eastern bound or western tide.
Upon these wonders great and small
The children of the earth may call,
But nothing can surpass the gain
That comes to one who would remain
Within the verdant tranquil space
Where peace and quiet both embrace
A dweller in the woods.

The forest has no walls to bind
The meditations of the mind.
There is no limit to the way
The forest has so much to say—
The windfall of the giant tree,

Still Waters

The buzzing of the bumblebee,
The meadow lush with summer flower,
The wind in treetops full of power.
Each of these communicates
And every moment inundates
A dweller in the woods.

This is surely not to say
That city life cannot be gay.
For business there is always done
From morning to the setting sun.
And people run both to and fro
Convinced that they are "in the know."
And that might be if truth were told,
For who would be so very bold
To say that city life is sad
Or that what happens there is bad?
A dweller in the woods!

It never would be said in spite
But rather to proclaim the plight
Of citizens both up and down
Whose only ties are to the town,
Who never have the chance to take

Still Waters

A walk where forest creatures make
The trails that humans seldom know
Through swamp or highland, rain or snow,
Who never hear the whippoorwill
Or other sounds that always thrill
A dweller in the woods.

So take me to the woods, my friend,
And let me stay there till the end,
Where rivers flow and lakes abound
And serenity for thought is found,
Where every morn a new day dawns
With views of mother deer and fawns,
And wild geese fly in autumn skies,
And snowflakes melt on wondering eyes,
And Nature's breast heaves with delight
When she embraces with her light
A dweller in the woods.

Still Waters

The Genealogist

Sometimes there strikes a person
Who is normal with desires—
A person who may otherwise
Be fairly free of error—
A bug that steals his reason
And his mind is turned to fires
That burn of family history
When before he didn't care.
Until this bug infects him—
Pursues its unrelenting goal—
He goes about his business
Every day with seeming ease.
But then he's overtaken
And the microbe fills his soul,
And he's not merely smitten
But he's fond of the disease.
He gives his full attention

Still Waters

To the study of the past.
You'll find him at the library
Reading films and dusty tomes
In the hope of finding tidbits
That his forebears might have cast
Until there's cause to wonder—
Does this person have a home?
The genealogist's pathology
Is benign in the beginning.
And subtle is its pathway
As it goes along its way,
Until the victim actually thinks
That he is somehow winning
In the great ancestral battle
That he wages every day.
The symptoms of this dread disease
Are easily defined—
The aching back, the weary eyes,
The constant thought process
Of sleuthing through the details
Of the lost he hopes to find.
Then headaches come and insomnia,
Till his whole life is a mess.
But does this stop the endless search

Still Waters

For data that is lost?
Not on your life, you may be sure,
For the research must go on.
For the missing tree (or bush or lawn)
Must be found at any cost,
Until the last dry leaf or blade
Of history has been won.
The genealogist's compulsive need
For names and dates and faces
Makes the patient go about
With the blankest of expressions
In search of all the latter things
As well as all the places
Where the ancients gained or lost
Or where they made concessions.
He is always writing letters
And their answers are anticipated
As the patient watches nervously
For deliveries at the mailbox.
And he thinks the mailman is a villain
And his service overrated,
While he schemes and plots his strategy
And thinks himself a fox.
There are no ointments, salves and powders,

Still Waters

Or other medications
For the disease of genealogists,
But the future may look brighter
Despite the many setbacks
And the sea of complications.
For if nothing else can be said of him
The genealogist is a fighter.
Give him some bit of information—
A date, a place, a name—
And the mindset of the patient
Takes a wholly different track.
Then on he goes refueled and strong
To fully play the game.
He thinks, he writes, he waits, he schemes,
And takes another tack.
But in the end, as time will tell
The patient does have hope.
His family always looks at him
With sympathy and love.
They know that his prognosis will improve
In time's vast scope,
And they thank him for his efforts
Praying blessings from above.
As for his work, there's nothing

Still Waters

*That another can replace.
And there's not a single note or word
That anyone would knock,
For his contribution and his cause
Are clearly done with grace.
And in the end he carves his name
On the great ancestral block.*

Part Two

Christmas

Still Waters

A Boy's Christmas

I.

When I was three, there used to be
At Christmas time my family,
With Mom and Dad and sisters, too,
And brothers big with things to do
Like take me out to watch them ski,
Or Dad would bounce me on his knee
And tell me tales of deer and bear
And catching rabbits in a snare.
I used to like to play a game;
It almost drove my mom insane.
My brother called it "Fox and Wizard."
It was always fun right after a blizzard
When the snow was soft and deep and white
After working hard all through the night
With silent magic thus to place
Upon the ground a perfect face

Still Waters

Without a blemish, spot or sore,
Or hint of what was there before,
While we were cozied up and warm
In our log house, away from the swarm
Of blowing winds and bitter cold—
Those things that make the grownups old.
As I was saying, there was this game.
It was always fun and never the same.
As Wizard, I would hide my eyes
(It often took me several tries),
While Fox would run and make his lair
Beneath a snowdrift large somewhere.
And I would try to find him when
I'd counted slowly up to ten.
I'd track him where he'd left a path,
And dig him out and then we'd laugh
And play some more till the sun was set,
And we, of course, were soaking wet.
And then we'd have to go inside,
And Mom was almost sure to chide
Us for the foolish thing we'd done,
But we were only having fun.
And so was she in her own way—
She liked to know she had her say.

Still Waters

But she remembered, too, no doubt,
The way she played when school was out,
Or thought about the time when she
Was small and only three like me.
When I was three, the Christmas tree
And all the gifts that were for me
Were really all that I could see—
The Tinker Toys and Lincoln Logs—
No kitty-cats or puppy-dogs,
I wanted some, but I was told
They didn't like it in the cold—
So a furry cap with muffs to match,
And my old blanket with the brand new patch,
Some hand-knit socks, a pair of skates,
And a puzzle of the United States
I found beneath the tree when I was three.
My Christmas was a time for glee.
I did not ask why Jesus came
To heal the sick, the blind, the lame.
Of babies born in mangers far,
Or if Dad bought another car,
It sounded all the same to me.
My world was small when I was three,
And everyone was tall as tall,

Still Waters

'Cuz I was small, when I was three.

II.
Then Christmas came when I was ten.
I found that things were different then.
The gifts and tree were as before,
But what I saw was so much more.
And what I saw, I must confess
In many ways was so much less.
This Christmas time I was confused.
The games and toys would go unused.
To every question I sought an answer:
Why was Daddy dying with cancer?
And when he died where would he go?
Of heaven and hell what did I know?
Within my little heart I cried.
And with my utmost strength I tried
To find some peace within the folly
Of "deck the halls with boughs of holly."
While the grownups talked of Reds and power,
Or campaigned hard for Eisenhower,
I recalled the Bethlehem manger,
And saw the more immediate danger
Of living without my dad to face

Still Waters

The world—a dark and dismal place.
The words would echo in my brain
To "Silent Night" and every strain
Of "Hark the Herald Angels Sing,"
And "Glory to the newborn king."
The Christmas tree when I was three
Wrought happiness and peace for me.
But visions of an awesome dread,
Not sugarplums dancing in my head,
Displaced the tinsel and the toys
Which seemed to be for other boys.
I did not find my peace that year,
But somehow knew I had come near,
Because there was within my soul
A restlessness to reach the goal
Of finding meaning in this life
Amidst the struggle and the strife,
Amidst the doubt and painful sorrow,
Amidst the questions of tomorrow.
I did not know that at the time
There was a greater joy sublime
For which I searched in everything,
Till I was sought out by the King.

Still Waters

III.

At twenty-one, when Christmas came
The boy was gone, but in his name
A man was found redeemed by grace
To tell the news in every place
That God had planned to shed the blood
Of his own son, so that the flood
Of all his love and kindness could
Become the share of all who would
Believe the mystery that the birth
Of Jesus surely must be worth
Whatever price it cost the Father
To rescue sinners all who bother
To bear his cross and take his side,
To slay each dawn their sinful pride.
At twenty-one, the voice was clear
And gently whispered in my ear:
"I left my heavenly home above
To humbly serve My Father's love,
To do His will in heart and mind
So you and those like you might find
The answers to your questing hearts
And oneness in your many parts.
So you the peace of God might know

Still Waters

And then with sacred purpose go
To give new meaning to the phrase:
"The Lord be with you all your days.'"
The years slip by and with each one
Another Christmas season's done.
The Christmas tree when I was three
No longer fills my heart with glee.
The present now beneath the Tree
Is quite a different one, you see.
It is the gift I choose to make.
There's nothing more for me to take.
A pilgrim to the manger scene,
I bring my life and by that mean
To let the Savior's incarnation
Be my daily inspiration.
I place myself beneath his Tree—
The One who bled and died for me—
The very best that I can bring
For Jesus, Master, God, and King.
Just let my eyes be on His face,
To always stay within His grace
Is what I ask this Christmas time.
This is the greatest joy sublime.
The years will come, the years will go;

Still Waters

But this one thing I surely know—
Beyond this life of gain or loss
There is a future in the cross.

Still Waters

Christmas Now

I.

I have described in other lines
The Christmases of former times,
When I was just a child of three
And Christmas was a time of glee
With tinsel, lights, and lots of toys,
And other things for little boys.
The years dragged on till I was ten.
Life made me feel much older then,
For I had learned that Dad was dying
I could not stop my heart from crying.
Then suddenly the years flew by,
There wasn't time to wonder why.
I earned degrees through much hard labor.
Education was my savor.
I studied music first of all.
I thought it was the highest call.

Still Waters

But soon I turned to other things,
Like Baggins searching for the rings.
Languages became my passion,
Semitic tongues of every fashion.
Ancient texts impressed on clay
Became the mainstay of my day—
Akkadian and Nuzi, too,
Every dialect through and through.
Grammar and syntax, tick by tick,
In Hebrew, Arabic and Ugaritic
I gave myself to hour by hour,
Living in the ivory tower.
All these tongues were learned and taught,
Until some other things I sought.

II.

So to the business world I turned,
Without my passion wholly spurned.
I still read languages at night,
But sales became my daily fight.
For food was needed on the table,
Sufficient income sure and stable.
And so the years passed one by one
Until my labors all were done.

Still Waters

And through it all I've had a life
Supported by a loving wife
Who sacrificed her dreams as well
In ways that I can scarcely tell.
But still our greatest hopes and joys
Are centered in our handsome boys,
For they are more than life or treasure,
And I love them beyond measure.
Our family now enlarged has grown
Grandchildren, too, we happily own
As priceless wonders in our hearts—
The whole is greater than the parts.
There's no replacing what I've got,
For what they give cannot be bought.
For all the good things that we share,
I'm grateful that my family's there.
To put it plainly in a word,
I'm lacking nothing that is good.

III.

All this is writ so I can say
What Christmas means to me this day.
I surely am so greatly blessed,
Much more it seems than all the rest,

Still Waters

Though not for things that I have done.
My gains I owe all to the Son
Whose birth still thrills me with delight,
Who lives on still though out of sight.
The Son of God remains the key
To the life that he has given me.
It's true, I've worked and sweat and toiled
And tried some things that I have spoiled,
But in the end I come to this:
There is no greater joy or bliss
By which a man can fully face
This life without a touch of grace.
It's grace that makes this Christmas grand.
It's grace whereon I take my stand.
It's grace that made the manger scene.
It's grace that makes the sinner clean.
Regardless of the time of life,
It's grace that conquers pain and strife.
I cannot say it well enough,
It's grace we need, not more of stuff.
It's grace we need because it's love
That God has shown us from above.
So if you ask me what to say
In summary of this Christmas day,

Still Waters

I'd say it's simple but it's true.
There is a gift awaiting you.
It is a gift that I have found,
A simple gift and yet profound,
Not beneath a Christmas tree,
But taken just the same for free.
It's grace, and for no other reason
I celebrate the Christmas season.

Still Waters

Marching Pilgrims

Rejoice, O Pilgrim, on your journey,
Though your path is rough and steep.
Lift your voice in song triumphant.
Now is not the time to weep.
Hear the trumpets and the drummers
Of the heavenly marching band.
See how high they hold their heads now
As they pass the Judge's stand.
Is the song they play familiar?
Have you heard it all before?
Every step is split precision.
They have memorized the score.
And behind them is the choir,
Every word sung loud and grand.
All together they are singing
"Marching to the Promised Land."
Surely you have heard this chorus,
Know the words and know the beat.

Still Waters

It was heard the very first time
At the newborn Savior's feet:
"We are lost and lonely pilgrims
Wandering through the darkest night.
Storm and cold prevailed against us,
And there was no hope in sight.
Stalking us without our weapons,
Like a lion in the wood,
All around us raged an evil
Greater than the common good.
Then we saw the blessed Savior
Born to bring us peace and love.
Immanuel, our God, is with us,
Sent to earth from heaven above.
Hosanna, now, O Pilgrim travelers,
Let us raise our song to sing
Praise unto the Lord eternal
Prophet, Priest, and mighty King."
Motivated by the witness
Of the pilgrims gone before,
Let us bear in mind the Promise
As we march toward heaven's door.
Ours is just a fleeting moment
That we spend upon this earth.

Still Waters

Yonder is our home forever,
Sponsored by the Savior's birth.
Rejoice, O Pilgrim, on your journey.
Celebrate this Christmas time.
For the Savior came to bring us
Life abundant and sublime.

Still Waters

The Journey

Wise men made their way encumbered
By the windblown desert sands.
From the East their journey led them
With their tribute in their hands.
Sandled Bedouin, full of wonder
At the star that led their way,
Came to Bethlehem that evening,
Came because of Christmas Day.
Did they know that God had entered
Into this world's time and space
In the form of yonder infant
Sheltered in that humble place?
What provoked them to their travels,
Leaving friends and homes behind?
What did fortune have before them?
What did they expect to find?
Driven by their intuition,
Guided by the stars above,

Still Waters

Came the wise men to the manger,
Came to see the Son of Love,
Knelt before Him ancient sages,
Great men at the baby's feet,
At the cradle of the Master
Where the East and West would meet,
Rose before Him from their worship,
Turned their faces to the East,
Learned in one important lesson:
"He is first and I am least."
Faith returned the Eastern wise men
To the place from whence they came,
Changed because they made the journey,
Made it in the Savior's name.

Still Waters

The First Christmas

From the distance time has fallen,
When the world was dark and void,
When the voice of God contoured it
To the purpose he employed,
Fallen through the ages endless,
Before the race could read or write,
When no flame had been invented
To warm and light eternal night.
Darkness wrapped the world external.
Mankind lived much like the beasts.
Then the voice of God invited
Adam's race to bounteous feasts:
"All the trees within the Garden
Are sufficient for your meat.
Fruit for you and all your children
Will be yours and theirs to eat.
But for one within the center
I have set apart from thee.

Still Waters

Do not eat its fruit forbidden,
Lest you die and anger me."
Eden's story has its ending
In the trail of human strife.
Enter death to Adam's children
When the Lord had promised life.
Now the world lies worn and suffering
Day by day its painful woes,
Night by night no salve or ointment
Where the man of darkness goes.
But another chapter written
By the God of grace and love
Gives the world another option
Illustrated by the Dove:
"I will send to you a Savior
Who will die for all your sins.
Only trust him to deliver,
And my peace will dwell within.
Come to me and I will feed you.
I will quench your endless thirst.
Life comes through the Second Adam
Just as death came by the first."
Immanuel has come to free us
From the sin and death we share.

Still Waters

Through his birth a hope is kindled.
By his life and death we care.
Advent is our time to listen
To the voice of God within,
Calling us to Jesus' cradle,
Freeing us from death and sin.
Take a moment to consider
Where your life is heading now.
Ask the Savior to forgive you.
Do not fear or question how.
Let this Christmas be your entrance
To the life he has in store.
And may all your days be happy
Through next year and many more.

Part Three

Inspiration

Still Waters

The Seed

There is a shadow large and eerie
In the land where I was born.
Every living thing is burdened
With a heavy heart forlorn.
No one noticed how the shadow
Grew upon us day by day,
Until the sullen darkness
Took the sunshine all away.
It is said that in an era
When the creatures walked in light,
A seed was sown by forces
That were meant to cause a blight.
Soon all the plants were smothered
That provided food and shade,
And weeds choked out the flowers
In the gardens men had made.
A short time passed and mighty winds
Transported evil seeds

Still Waters

Around the globe to every place
And turned it into weeds.
Nothing could be done
Against the flow of harm and vice,
So a flood was sent to stop it
And the flood was turned to ice.
Still the pestilence endangered
Every species on the earth,
Every plant and every mammal
That had ever given birth.
So a fire was sent to kill it
But that failed, too, in its turn,
For the seed was of a substance
That would not begin to burn.
Some men were sent to fight the seed
And end the awful plague.
They warned against the danger
But their messages were vague.
So the people sat in silence
As the seed was spread abroad,
And they failed to see their error
When they finally called it god.
Now the earth is locked in darkness
And awaits another day

Still Waters

When the sorrow of the ages
Will be fully wiped away.
All hope is for the moment,
In the twinkling of an eye,
When the present age expires
And the evil seed will die.

Still Waters

The Gallery

It's silent now, the hour is past
When sinister shadows grimly cast
Their darkness o'er my soul.
In marble halls of lighted space
The artist longed his work to place,
To realize his goal.
So long he worked with gentle hands,
Like ocean waves upon the sands,
And no cost did he spare.
As form and line the master drew,
His vision for the gallery grew,
Till nothing was left bare.
His genius was clear throughout.
Each masterpiece without a doubt
Was perfect in its place.
He marked each piece with His own name,
Endorsing it with all his fame,
And filled it with his grace.

Still Waters

At last the final stroke was made.
The drapes were placed to give their shade.
His tools were laid aside.
The artist viewed the work he'd done
And knew the task was just begun,
And then the master died.
The shrouds removed, I came to see
The master's plan revealed to me.
My heart was black as coal.
It's silent now, the hour is past
When sinister shadows grimly cast
Their darkness o'er my soul.

Still Waters

The Creation

I.

"In the beginning God created. . ."
In this summation it is stated
That the derivation of the earth,
And matters all of any worth,
Including life in every region,
Animals and plants in legion,
Do not exist by happenstance
Or any other circumstance,
But we are made to understand
By nothing but divine command.
Of course this statement is debated,
By some denied and some gold-plated.
The critic says, "How can it be?
For science teaches that the sea
Gave birth to life and then ensued
A process that for long pursued
Development to a higher state.

Still Waters

And to this process man came late.
The fittest of them all survived
And by reason of his brain derived
The tools he needed to sustain
His power o'er subdued terrain.
'Creation' is a natural progress
From the simple to the complex.
That is how man came to be.
His origin is in the sea."

II.

The faithful, on the other hand,
Insist upon their own demand:
"That is not how we came to be.
We are not children of the sea.
We did not start as plankton then
In time our vertebrae begin
To form, and then our bones took shape
Like fins to fan the oceanscape.
Our lungs, not gills, provide the air
We breathe and better still, how fair
And fine to us are thoughts of love—
Surely these are from above.
'As a child I was a fish'

Still Waters

Is nothing more than just a wish
Of those who cannot face the claim
That God made man in his own frame."

III.

What matters great in this debate
Is how mankind has learned to hate.
To some, man's source is evolution.
His problems all have that solution.
Others claim that revelation
Only gives the explanation.
And between these two extremes
There seem to be no common means
To bridge the gulf created by
Divergent views of knowing why.
And so we cannot deal with how
To live in peace both here and now.

Still Waters

God's Promise

Strong beyond all measure
Is the one who trusts in me.
Nothing can remove him
From my constant company.
Life will bring its hardships.
Each day may fill with care.
Just know that I am with you
And I always will be there.
I see your present sorrow.
I stand by to treat your pain.
For I am the Great Physician
And they are only for your gain.
Life is evanescent,
And death will have its way.
But I have made provision
For an everlasting day.
Never doubt that I am with you.
You will never be alone.

Still Waters

For your angel's here to witness
That I'm still upon my throne.
My power will sustain you.
My grace will long endure.
My love is everlasting.
Of that you can be sure.
I have prepared a place for you.
I cannot tell you how.
But one is waiting to receive you
For your angel's with me now.
I took her from you early,
Though I could have healed her, son.
I took her from you early
Because her work was done.
But your work is still unfinished
So be steadfast and be strong.
Do not be disheartened,
Though the nights are dark and long.
I will lead you. I will guide you.
Never fail to trust in me.
For I will be your captain
On the ever raging sea.
Stay the course until you're finished
With the work you have to do,

Still Waters

While your angel's here rejoicing
And watching over you.
Let your joy come in the morning
When your night of grief has passed.
Set your mind upon the future
And the things that always last.
Rise up and be my witness
Of what you've seen and heard.
Tell the story of my kindness
As you find it in my Word.
So that all may know the fullness
Of the promise that I give:
"Abide in me as I in you,
Then forever you will live."

Still Waters

The Heart of God

There is a place where sorrows old
Will seem as if they're made of gold,
Where memories of a hurtful past
Will never more than seconds last—
It is the heart of God.
We all will travel trails of pain
Where thunderstorms and drenching rain
Would all but tear us from our way
And make us even farther stray
Beyond the heart of God.
Beyond the storms are sunny days
With brighter thoughts and better ways.
Our pain and sorrow are the key
That other folks may someday see
More plain the heart of God.
So many times our hearts have died.
So many times our eyes have cried
Great tears because of hurts we know.

Still Waters

But these are seeds which planted grow
Within the heart of God.
Our minds are but a sacred mirror
For hopes and dreams as well as fear.
The images reflected there,
If shrouded by a veil of prayer,
Will touch the heart of God.
Be gone, dark night of sorrows past.
The morning light is coming fast
To lift our spirits bright and high,
Because our Christ is standing nigh
Beside the heart of God.
A quiet place we now have found
On firmer, safer, higher ground.
We rest assured because God's grace
Enables us to fix our faith
Upon the heart of God.

Still Waters

Horizons

There is a land where dreams come true,
Where aspirations old and new
Are realized by but a few
Who dare to make the move.
Like Israel on the Moab plains,
This move is not without its pains,
But the land of promise still remains
To those who make the move.
The obstacles are great and tall,
Like giants standing one and all,
But no ill fate will e'er befall
The one who makes the move.
The voices from the other side,
Where souls departed now abide,
Cry "Blessings great and multiplied
For those who make the move."
It is an act of solemn will
That drives the weary pilgrim till

Still Waters

She sees the hope beyond the hill
For those who make the move.
A pioneer in faith, she makes
One step and then another takes,
And soon behind her all forsakes
And dares to make the move.
The land before her now is flung.
Its milk and honey song is sung.
A life anew is now begun.
For one who made the move.

Still Waters

A Better Day

Whenever you're down in the dumps,
Consider what I say.
At least you haven't got the mumps!
Today's a better day!
If blues is what you're having now,
Consider what I say.
Just think about a laughing cow!
Today's a better day!
When your days are filled with stress,
Consider what I say.
There's always someone who has less.
Today's a better day!
If you've been overcome with grief,
Consider what I say!
Time's by far the greater thief.
Today's a better day!
When all you do is question why,
Consider what I say.

Still Waters

Look up! The sun's still in the sky!
Today's a better day!
When you're feeling all alone,
Consider what I say.
God's still in heaven on his throne.
Today's a better day!
So sadness and despair release.
Consider what I say.
And let your heart be filled with peace.
Today's a better day!

Still Waters

A Worm And Her Majesty

I.

"While upon this earth I crawl,
Humbly to Thy face I call
Not knowing when or whence
I came or what I shall be hence.
In my present circumstances,
Part by choice and part by chances,
I am but a lowly peasant
Yearning for a life more pleasant.
From leaf to leaf I labor daily,
Always burdened, never gaily.
Is this the only life for me,
Devouring earth, tree by tree?
Surely from Thy high position,
Thou canst see my dire condition.
Canst Thou tell me, is there hope
Beyond my narrow, dismal scope?"

Still Waters

II.

"I am not some distant fairy,"
Spoke the Monarch to this query.
"Real as real I sit beside you.
From this branch I too will guide you.
For once I was just as you are,
From my condition just as far.
The route I took from that to this
Is known as metamorphosis.
You have begun to make a start.
That yearning deep within your heart,
If nurtured properly will grow
Until one day my form you know.
It is by choice and not by chances
That you change your circumstances.
Who you are and what you do
Is in the end all up to you."

III.

"Monarch Royal," asked the Lowly,
"Does it happen fast or slowly?
Does it hurt or is it painless?
Is there blood or is it stainless?"
"It is a process," said Her Highness.

Still Waters

"Pain there is and times of dryness.
If blood there be upon your brow,
Would you be better off than now?
There is a price that must be paid—
 Your life upon the altar laid.
 To learn to live you have to die.
 I cannot give you reasons why.
 If fear dissuades you on the way,
 It is as worm that you will stay.
 But if by faith you come to die,
 You will become a butterfly.

IV.

 The Monarch lifted to the sky
 And left the lowly worm to cry.
 Up and up Her Highness soared,
 While Worm continued to be bored.
 "What shall I be, what shall I do?"
 The hapless caterpillar stewed.
 "I'll never learn to flit and fly.
 My life is merely passing by.
 For all I do is eat and sleep,
 Complain a lot and then I weep.
 I cannot stand another day

Still Waters

Of living in this awful way."

V.

A long time passed until the worm
Grew tired of longing and concern
About the future and the past
And what she'd do that would always last.
So, full of leaves she found a twig,
About her size or twice as big,
Where she could sit and think and rest
Until her world changed for the best.
Down below her on the ground,
People passed and children found
Their games to play like hide and seek.
(She noticed how they liked to peek.)
Then in the wind she felt a chill.
She took a leaf and wrapped until
Her body was enclosed completely,
Like a mummy sealed so neatly.
Warm and cozy in this station
She gave up on contemplation.
Instead she turned her thoughts to bed,
Recalling what the Monarch said.

Still Waters

VI.

When Worm awoke, the day was bright
And the Monarch was in sight,
Flying free and tasting flowers
Fresh from early morning showers.
His course came near the old oak tree
Where Worm had spent her reverie.
Each graceful movement in his wings
Stirred Worm to think the strangest things.
She began to feel that she could fly
As Monarch once again passed by.
Her heart began to pound with gladness.
She laid aside her former sadness.
Suddenly she left her bed,
Stood straight up and cleared her head.
That's when the Monarch saw her there
And landed on the oak branch where
He could get a closer look
At Worm. And then he took
His wing and raised it high,
Saluting something in the sky,
And off he lifted from the tree
As he beckoned Worm: "Come fly with me."

Still Waters

Tadpole Yearnings

I am just a tadpole waiting
Long to be a frog.
I often think of something great,
Like sitting on a log.
I want to feel the sun's warm rays
Directly on my back
And jump along the muddy bank
Where I could leave a track.
It's hard for me to comprehend
How free a frog must be,
And even harder to believe
That a frog is really me.
The way of Nature puzzles me
And leaves me all befuddled
As to why the frog is running free
And I am always puddled.
Rumors float around the pond
And like lily pads abound,

Still Waters

Saying tadpoles have potential
To be walking on the ground.
Riddles have their hidden secrets
That their tellers will not give,
But how can tadpoles ever hope
To change the way they live?
I hear the frogs a-croaking
As the twilight dims the day,
And I know that I could learn their songs
If I could find a way
To change my form and leave the pond
To live the way they do.
But now I wait and sometimes think
My dreams will not come true.
But just as surely as my hopes
Are dampened by my clime,
I know deep down that Nature's plan
Is perfect and sublime.
My time will come not when I choose
But when the time is right,
And then I'll leave my tadpole friends
And live where life is bright.
From tadpole status to a frog
I certainly will grow.

Still Waters

Whatever life can offer
On the land I'll surely know.
I realize that time is
Of the essence for my cure.
I also know for certain
That my destiny is sure.
And so I daily wait and swim
And think and watch and pray,
And hold on fast to what I think,
No matter what they say.
For other tadpoles seem so lost
Without a ray of hope
And struggle through their daily lives
Within their narrow scope.
But one day I will show them
That my time has really come.
And dawn will also come for them
(At least that's true for some).
Then all together we'll rejoice
And sing and hop along,
And then we'll know without a doubt
That we're just where we belong.

Still Waters

What Have You Done For Me?

What shall we lay before God's throne
When yonder bridge we cross?
The earthly gains assembled now
Will then be counted loss.
How empty will our labors seem
When time shall be no more.
What shall we carry with us
When we enter heaven's door?
One question will be asked of us
When Jesus Christ we see.
The Savior will confront us with
"What have you done for me?
I note your education and
The businesses you led.
The real estate you purchased
And the family that you fed.
These things are noble ventures
And fulfilling in their way.

Still Waters

But did you take the time you had
To meditate and pray?
I see you traveled round the globe
To visit distant lands.
And soaked in summer sunshine
On their seas and on their sands.
Of course there is a need to
Rest the body and the mind.
But in your many travels, what
Of my peace did you find?
A world of lost humanity
I placed beside your door:
The wealthy and the arrogant,
The wretched and the poor.
Like sheep without a shepherd,
They had wandered all astray.
But did you preach the gospel
To illuminate their way?
I came to earth to pay the price
To ransom every soul.
My blood was shed upon the cross
To make the world whole.
The message of salvation was
Entrusted to your hands.

Still Waters

Did you find the time to teach it,
Or had you other plans?
Important as they might have been,
They're all behind you now.
It doesn't matter what they were
Or when or why or how.
One thing remains beyond the rest
When you face eternity.
I the put the question to you now—
What have you done for me?"

Still Waters

Trees

We are as trees, the sky apart,
From tender roots we take our start
And struggle through uncultured soil
Toward unknown destination.
The sky lifts not, we push our way
Inch by inch through stubborn clay
Until we feel within our hearts
A growing inspiration.
'Tis not for us to live as moles,
Confined to subterranean holes.
Roots do not define us all.
There is a higher station.
We wait and wait until it's time
To germinate, to grow, to climb,
To leave behind our shuttered state
For another orientation.
Our heads held high, our hearts intact,
We break the ground in one proud act

Still Waters

And sense the warmth upon our pates
From Sol's illumination.
Darkness now behind us lies.
We lift our hands to vaulted skies
And drink the air into our lungs
In sudden transformation.
Although constrained against our will,
Our buried dreams define us still.
With diligence we stay our course
Without a reservation.
Our roots remain secure and sound
Beneath the surface of the ground,
While we must chart in this new world
A course of navigation.
At first we find it hard to face,
Like aliens from another place,
The changing elements, the snow,
The cold precipitation.
We learn that change is part of life.
Although it comes through pain or strife,
We trust our roots to hold us fast
Through storm or conflagration.
We look to left and look to right
And drive unguided through the night

Still Waters

Of darkness that enfolds the world
In constant consternation.
Hope swells within our hearts and then
It ebbs away without our ken,
But still we reach to bring it near
By our imagination.
Upward, upward is our climb,
A millimeter at a time.
Imperceptibly we grow
Through strong determination.
To what great purpose is a tree?—
We ask ourselves in maturity—
To stand and wait while others serve
And bear humiliation?
Some lovers pass and carve their names,
And children stop to do the same.
How insignificant life seems,
Of worth a violation.
We finally come to realize,
To reach our dreams and other highs,
We cannot do so on our own
Without regeneration.
The birds build homes within our boughs,
Our branches shelter grazing cows,

Still Waters

And nature moves around us now
Without communication.
And with the years we older grow,
But no more heights we seem to know,
And every day goes by the same—
A wooden machination.
We cast our seeds upon the thrust
Of wind that carries off our trust.
Our children sprout, then grow like us—
Another generation.
What will they be? What will they do?
Our worried bark is furrowed through.
All our hopes and dreams are wrapped
In pure exasperation.
We learn we can't do otherwise,
The years have somehow made us wise.
We cannot live our lives through them—
A brilliant observation.
So back the question comes again,
Like music of an endless strain.
What is the purpose of a tree?—
Our self-interrogation.
A silent voice within reveals,
"It is not yours to break the seals.

Still Waters

By faith believe what God conceals,"—
A noble revelation.
"There is a point where compromise
Will not put up with further lies.
It's then you find within your heart
A quiet consolation.
But ultimately, that's not all.
The time will come when you must fall
And give your life unselfishly—
A perfect immolation.
From you a host of things will be,
But in the meantime be a tree,
And leave your destiny to me—"
God's final declaration.
Despite our best attempts to gain
The freedom that will keep us sane,
There always comes another time
For utter aggravation.
The seasons come, the seasons go.
The challenges of life we know.
But in the end we take our stand
With rising aspiration.
The morning breaks, a new day starts,
We wake to learn and play new parts.

Still Waters

The past we leave behind us now
For greater approbation.
We hear God's voice, we seek his face,
We know that there's another place
To which we'll go when day is done—
Our final elevation.

Still Waters

Voices

I heard the call of distant voices,
Nondescript in what they said.
It was as though they spoke in silence,
Like the voices of the dead.
I listened long to parse their syntax,
To find a message hidden there.
But I could not take the measure
Of the voices—how or where.
They seemed a mere, untidy jumble,
Like a far off, stormy rumble,
Growing fainter as I wondered
What was said or what was thundered.
They seemed like colors from a palette
Mixed together with a mallet
By a painter now gone crazy.
The distant voices were so hazy.
But since I was not used to voices
Speaking to me in this way,
I was help in rapt attention

Still Waters

When I finally heard them say:
"Achulamapucu poco."
Then they paused a moment long—
"Sotto melo mocho lono."
It was as though they made a song.
If there was meaning in the message,
I could not cipher it at all.
But just as nails need a hammer,
I was destined for the call.
So I began to mull it over.
Then a rhythmic beat was heard,
Until I found that I could sing it
Sotto voce word by word.
Soon the far off distant voices
That I'd heard some time before
Became my voice in song triumphant
As I sang it more and more.
Still I did not understand
The meaning of each given phrase,
But the song revived my spirit
And it lasted several days.
What is language? What is meaning?
If not the voices that you find

Still Waters

Although obscure and often hidden
Within the walls of your own mind.
Now I take the time to listen
To the voices that I hear,
Even when their sound is silent,
And their message is unclear.

Still Waters

A Humble Prayer

In the morning will I seek Thee,
Ere the business of the day
Like a bandit with a Bowie
Robs me of the time to pray.
Gracious Savior who has taught us
That the crowd is not the place,
Meet me in a quiet corner
Where I humbly seek Thy face.
I would be Thy faithful servant
Every day and every hour.
Fill me, Lord, and energize me
With Thy everlasting power.

Still Waters

The Giant Self

Today is your day. It is my gift to you. What you do with it is your pleasure. I will not interfere. You have the power to choose to make this day the best day of your life. As long as what you choose is in harmony with the songs that are sung by your giant self, you cannot fail nor can you be condemned, even by those who would misunderstand you from their own lack of insight into their private space. You are in charge of your world. This is your day. Make the most of it, and during the night hours I will celebrate with you the progress you are making in harmonizing with me. I am your giant self. I am your truest friend.

Still Waters

Sunset

Golden disc beyond the reach of man,
Ever sinking to rise again
To find us where we are not now
Nor where we can be.
The eye beholds what it knows not.
Beauty falls off the earth and remains yet
Where it cannot be seen
Until the light appears once more.
Beneath this world is this world.
Endless striving finds only what is always there.
Before life comes death, before light darkness,
And the dawn is before and after,
For the dawn is of sunset born.